LOVER'S CURSE

LIFE TURNS AWAY FROM ME, AND DEATH DENIES ME TOO, TELL ME, WHERE AM I TO GO. THESE ARE NOTHING BUT TRACES OF YOU

ADITI BHANDARI

Made with ♥ on the Notion Press Platform
www.notionpress.com

DEDICATION

For every heart that has loved, lost, and quietly endured,

THIS IS FOR YOU....

To every soul that has loved, lost, and risen anew, to the dreamers who find solace in words, and to the broken hearts that still dare to beat. To the quiet warriors who battle the storms within, to the lovers who dared to give their hearts, even when it hurt, and to the dreamers who craft beauty from pain. This book is for you. May these verse be a gentle companion to your joys, a mirror to your sorrows, and a light in the darkest corners of your soul.

To my readers:

Each poem here is a peice of my soul, a reflection of love, loss, and the enduring hope for brighter tomorrows.

With time- Broken bones will mend, But
broken heart will not heal, Learn to live with
it...

Contents

Contents

Lover's Curse

Foreword

I feel incredibly proud to introduce my best friend's art to the world. Hey everyone! I'm Judo [nickname] Aditi's best friend. I love that Aditi's poetry speaks directly to the heart, capturing love, loss, and resilience with stunning clarity. I deeply admire how she never gave up, channeling her boundless passion into every word she writes. Her steadfast dedication shines through, making this collection truly extraordinary.

It's a privilege to introduce this work, a reflection of her talent and soul.

Dear Readers you should go for it.

-Judo

Preface

Every teardrop carries a story. Every sigh holds a secret. And every broken heart leaves behind echoes that resonate in the quiet spaces of our lives. This book is a collection of those stories, those secrets, and those echoes—woven together in verse.

The poems within these pages are born from the depths of love, the pain of heartbreak, and the resilience of the human spirit. They reflect moments of vulnerability, longing, and healing, capturing emotions that words often fail to express.

Hey everyone out there! I'm the author of this book. Writing these poems has been both a catharsis and a revelation for me. They were written in times when my heart sought answers, comfort, or simply a way to feel heard. I hope that as you read them, you'll find pieces of your own journey within the lines—whether it's the thrill of first love, the ache of goodbye, or the quiet strength that comes after the storm.

This book is my offering to anyone who has ever loved deeply, lost profoundly, hopeless.

IMPORTANT

At the heart of this collection lies a theme that speaks to those who have experienced the pain of loss, whether it's the absence of a loved one or the bittersweet endings in stories we hold dear. To those who find solace in the fictional worlds of dramas, Marvel, or Spider-Man, this book is for you too. The emotions we feel for characters and heroes are as real as our own, reminding us of the beauty and fragility of connections, both real and imagined.

Prologue

Love begins like a sunrise—warm, radiant, and full of promise. It fills the heart with laughter, joy, and the thrilling innocence of shared dreams. But as the light dances, shadows begin to emerge.

This collection of poems is a journey through the seven stages of love and loss. From the bubbly elation of first love to the quiet heartbreak of misunderstandings. From playful banter to the silence of isolation. From the hope of reconciliation to the despair of hopelessness—and, ultimately, to the finality of goodbye.

And yet, at the heart of these emotions lies a deeper connection—a special theme for those who have loved and lost, for those who find themselves living stories of heartbreak in real life or fiction, and for those who cherish the bittersweet beauty of dramatic endings.

This book is not just about sorrow or joy—it is about the human spirit, navigating the ebb and flow of connection. As you turn the pages, may you find a reflection of your own journey and perhaps, the courage to embrace every facet of love, even the ones that hurt.

Welcome to the story of love, in all its beauty and pain.

With heartfelt gratitude,

Aditi

Acknowledgements

~ This book would not have been possible without the love, guidance, and support of so many people.

~ To my family, thank you for your unwavering belief in me and for standing by me through every step of this journey.

~ To my bestfriend, who cheered me on and listened to my endless ramblings about poems and themes, your encouragement means the world to me.

~ To my readers, especially those who've embraced my words and connected with my emotions, thank you for giving these poems a place in your hearts.

~ To the creators of the dramas, stories, and heroes that I cherish—from poignant Chinese dramas to Marvel's unforgettable worlds—thank you for inspiring me with tales that remind us of the beauty in every emotion.

~ And to life itself, for all the experiences—both joyous and heartbreaking—that have shaped me into who I am today. Thank you for teaching me to feel deeply, to grow through every trial, and to find beauty even in the most difficult moments.

Content Warning

This book explores deep and intense emotional themes, including self-harm, isolation, hopelessness, the will to not live, and reflections on the concept of a deathbed. These topics are handled with care but may be triggering for some readers.

If you are struggling with similar emotions, please know that you are not alone. Consider reaching out to someone you trust or a mental health professional for support. You are valued, loved, and deserving of help and healing.

Reader discretion is advised.

Important

Dear readers,

Thankyou for supporting my first poetry book. I sincerely apologize for any small mistakes or printing errors. Your understanding means so much to me as I grow on this journey.

Warm Regards,

Aditi

Contents

Special Theme
~ **Broken Strings**

1. ......

A love potion,

Just struck me in slow motion...

LOVE IN BLOOM

LOVE IN BLOOM

LOVE : Love Open Visions Expecting Tomorrow

LOVE

It's not just four words,

Love made me feel alive,

Made me yearn for tomorrow,

Love healed the wounds within,

And drew stars on my scars.

Love is everything that I never felt before,

As my life was only sore,

But now it's something more.

I wish for time to be forever frozen still,

So I could hold you onto the memories and love you at will...

MORNING DEW

The smile that seems to never leave,

The butterflies, growing that I believe.

You lit up my world,

A feeling so pure, I can't quite name.

The jolt of warmth when our hands meet,

A fleeting moment, yet so sweet.

When you're near, my heart's at ease,

Dancing lightly in the evening breeze.

My face in different shades of red, a few,

But then it fades away like morning dew.

At last, the butterflies flew...

SUNLIGHT

Your bubbly personality shines with pure vitality,

The sun's golden beam and your smile like a dream.

I think I'll run with you beside the ocean,

Our hearts alive with every motion.

Our love is in the air,

And the butterflies flare.

You dozing off over my shoulder,

And I want us to stay like this, growing older.

You are like the sunlight,

Endlessly bright, a guiding light...

DAYLIGHT

Some say love kills,

But here I stand, thriving in its warmth,

I am myself, yet a different me,

A reflection of the person I am with him.

The things my parents could never understand,

He comprehends without a single word—

"Together forever,"

When spoken by him, those words hold a beauty untold.

I see it clearly now,

Love is not what they promised.

I believed that love would be black and grey,

But it's warm and bright like a sun ray...

MIDNIGHT

You are sunlight, and I am the glow of night,

Once, I was midnight rain,

But now I am a peaceful plain.

Every time you touch me,

I drift into the butterfly sea.

I was in love before I even knew love's name...

2. ......

If you are the sun, then let me be your rays,

If you are the moon, let me be your light's embrace.

If you are the mirror, let me be your reflection,

Together, we are bound by silent connection...

RESONANCE OF YESTERDAY

RESONANCE OF YESTERDAY

HOLLOW ACHE

I'm so numb,

Even my mother's harsh words are dull echoes,

Fading in the hollow of my mind.

I trace fragile lines along my wrist,

As if in these soft curves, I might feel alive again.

Life seeps slowly from these lines,

carrying warmth— echoes of what I once held dear.

But they slip away, like whispers in the dark,

Leaving only faint red shadows behind.

Then I'm reaching for pieces of myself in those lines.

Trying to remember what it feels to be alive...

A WAY OUT

My parents are arguing in the other room,

While I sit quietly, feeling the gloom.

I'm trying to understand everyone in this house,

But it feels like I'm lost, like a quite mouse.

There is no one who makes an effort to understand me,

I'm left in the shadows longing to be free.

One text is all it takes,

For you to come and rescue me,

Not just from this house, but from a world unkind,

Where love is a ghost, and peace is blind...

THE STORM WITHIN YOU

You call it quits with your passion,

Leaving it all in the past, and the action.

You feel you're not a good son, not a good friend, not a good
boyfriend.

But what you don't know, boy, you're the best for me,

That's all that matters, can't you see?

You don't have to be perfect, your efforts alone make you worth it.

You're getting depressed by those who demotivate you,

But people are idiots, their opinions aren't true.

Your honey river eyes, I could drown in the sweetness of their ties.

Your silky hair,

The hoodies you wear,

The bubbly vibe you bear.

The way you keep making efforts, though you're worn out,

Shows strength in you, without a doubt...

DEJA VU

You say your hands are trembling, and I see your pain assembling.

It's not the same anymore, I see you struggling to the core.

I think I've been there too, I've been through.

I get déjà vu,

The same things that happened to me come into view.

Everyone's words, just a blur mumbling to my ears,

Then comes the tears.

The splash of blood that makes me feel alive,

The traces within them, I strive to survive.

I'm trying to calm you down, you're lost in your frown.

Heavy breaths, Twinkling tears,

A heart weighed down by fears.

You're fine, I whisper, hoping you'll never slip, sir.

As your sobs are now reducing, calm is slowly introducing...

3. ......

I'm staring at you, standing in a nice dress,

But your words cut me deep, leaving me with this nice mess...

BETWEEN US, UNSPOKEN

BETWEEN US, UNSPOKEN

FRAYED LINES

I never even realized when our small playful fights

turned into endless weeks of bitter arguments.

The once comforting rhythm of "We fight, we fix, we stay"

Changed into the cold indifference of

"We fight, we don't fix, we don't stay."

You screamed at me-knowing how much I break when voices rise,

Yet you let your anger drown my fragile cries.

The misunderstandings grew, and you, only let it screw.

You left, your anger lingering in the air,

And I stood there, too numb to repair.

Standing there picking up pieces of the broken glass,

And I let it leaves scars.

Lost in thoughts, where did I go wrong, but I'm too trying to be
strong...

BROKEN REFLECTION

I only just began to smile, but fate struck again,

Maybe I'm not worthy of love, or it's just the way you make me
feel within.

I tried to mend the rift between us, but you—

Only twisted it further, made it all fall through.

Voices screaming, glass shattering, hands in despair,

It became something we never wanted to share.

I'll still live with your name,

And die with the same...

SHATTERED SILENCE

You've somehow lost me somewhere,

Or perhaps I've lost myself.

As I stand at the end of a cliff that seems empty but has a lot inside it,

Just like my heart.

Wondering where has this love brought me to?

The leaf that falls from a tree, it will always remain.

Just like the love that causes through my veins.

Let me guard our broken dreams.

I accept that our love is incomplete,

Only what's unfinished remains alive.

Is love a game of cards to you??

Breaking and bending trust anew??

How long must the heart endure this silence??

COLOURED GLASS TEARS...

Long separations, tangled in my soul,

Oh Lord, why did you make love so cruel?

Breathless nights, a river of tears,

But not a single tear on my cheek appears.

My tears, like shattered glass, lost their hue,

Emotionless, they fall, but are still true.

Each tear holds a thousand silent pleas,

Fragments of a heart broken by memories,

Holding the moments I once held dear,

But now they fade, replaced by endless fear.

And all that remains, is beyond our reach...

4. ......

I hate watching our love go down in waves,

As it slips away, my heart still craves...

LOVE
IN
FLAMES

LOVE IN FLAMES

THE DROWNED MELODY

You're here in front of my door, apologizing till 8 PM,

Or is it just my thought?

I still have the gifts you bought,

Memories of what we once sought.

We're drenching in the rain together,

But now I'm drenching in my own tears, and it's nothing better.

Now my heart is burdened with your mistakes,

A heavy weight that never breaks.

I'm trying to erase the sorrows written by my fate,

But the past lingers on, I can't escape the weight...

DREAD HOPE..

You're tryna ghost me,

To leave me at a sea,

Lost in the waves,

Where no one can see.

I'm screaming,

My face buried in my pillow,

Feeling low.

Your promises, broken,

Now I'm left rotten,

I'm living incomplete,

Every sorrow tells me this,

I need you,

But you're the one I miss...

BLIND TO THE END

I'm still in love with you, I love you, it's true.

I'm sorry, my heart's confined—You're kind,

Yet sometimes unkind, I love you, I forgive you,

For ghosting me, for time undone,

For blaming me when words would run.

For leaving me when I begged you to stay,

For breaking promises along the way.

As sick as your actions sound, I loved you first .

I'm trying to make amends for things I didn't do,

I thought that's just the way life flows through.

But it haunts me, the love we could never be.

Remind me once more, how love feels, in your arms, where time heals.

I love you, I'm sorry,

My heart can't deny, You're all that I want, the reason I try...

THE SIN OF LOVE ...

Every sin bears the weight of its own reckoning.

And my sin? My sin is that I lost myself in love.

Too lost to find the words my heart would speak.

I'm still holding onto everything that's dead and gone,

wishing you were here, not just a memory drawn.

It was my fault for letting you get too close, yet I can't bring
myself to let you go.

Baby we're cursed but,

I'd let the world end for you, just to stand beside you.

Just to hear you calling out my name ...

5. ......

I never realized that falling in love and soaring in love were worlds apart...

UNTETHERED

UNTETHERED

LOVE FROM AFAR

How could I disturb your life,

When it blooms so perfectly without me?

The peace you cradle now,

Is the one my presence could never set free.

I wish to be near,

Yet loving you from afar feels almost too easy.

My heart whispers, "Stay,"

But my mind pleads, "Let go, don't be greedy."

So I drift away,

Like an autumn leaf, torn and worn—

Falling, never to return,

A quiet echo of love forlorn...

THE FALL

"Love kills," they warned—

But I leapt anyway,

Falling so hard, so deep,

There was no hope of recovery, only fragments of what I used to
be.

I'm amazed I'm still alive,

But I think I lost it.

Your presence lingers, haunting my every thought,

And our memories—ruthless, relentless—

Hunt me in the dark corners of my mind,

A cruel reminder of what love has taken away...

ETERNAL FADING SCARS

"My heart remembers every ache it endured,

Yet it fails to grasp the depth of the pain that left it numb."

"Loving someone more than myself left me with a heart too
scarred to love again."

I am tired of life, I'm not really happy but I don't wanna die.

I screeched, cried , begged and screamed for you to stay , but ,

Then I screeched, cried, begged and screamed to myself - to be
heartless

Even going out of the house was a torture to me.

Everywhere I looked, I saw us—wrapped up in each other,

Lost in love, clinging to something beautiful.

But now, I can't love anymore.

You took that part of me when you left, leaving my heart
somewhere I can't reach.

I feel anger, but even hate is empty,

Just like the love that used to burn so brightly. You stole that, too.

I'm still grieving on our separation but now I don't even wanna

meet.

Life drifts further from my grasp,

While death grows ever more ruthless in its pursuit.

I am alive but I am dead ...

BROKEN TIMELINES

The moment I realized I wanted to stay with him,

It was already too late.

We craved each other desperately,

Yet fate had cruelly cast us as the wrong people at the wrong time.

As the shadows of my demise closed in, I whispered softly,

"In another universe, my love,

We'll hold onto every promise we made.

But for now, let me go.

This life of mine is too hard."

And as my words faded into the void,

So did the last fragments of a love that could never be...

6. ......

Two lost souls, giving each other hope, creating a home...

You left me breathless with a nasty scar...

LOST WILL

LOST WILL

WANDERING HOPE

I never expected us to be perfect,

We were just two lost souls,

Trying to complete our goals,

Living each day in hope we'd make it out—

But what was it all about?

Tired of family, fake friends, and life,

Holding a knife,

Telling each other to hold on,

That our passion is still not gone...

SILENT CRIES..

I'm losing my will to live,

With nothing left to give.

Everyone thinks I don't care,

But here I am, crying my heart out in silence.

Thinking where I'm going wrong,

Sitting up tight at 2 AM,

Wishing for answers, but none come again.

But I guess my silence is my answer,

A quiet scream I can't transfer...

7. ......

Before you leave,

Just remember,

Someone is alive, holding on to the hope of you...

Alive
Yet
Ashes

ALIVE YET ASHES

TRACES OF YOU

Today someone asked about you, and I felt the sting of tears in my
eyes.

I miss everything we had.

I miss our late night talks, your way of soothing me with love.

You bringing me flowers my favourite little trinkets,

All those thoughtful surprises.

I miss every detail, every sweet gesture of yours, but I don't miss
you.

The way you loved me was just as perfect as,

The way you left me when I needed you the most.

I cherish our memories and the love we shared,

But I don't love you anymore.

Everything you gave me in love was just as perfect as the panic
attacks you left me with - back then, I didn't even knew what
panic attacks were.

Then came the days when I had to pat myself gently,

Trying to calm down,

Just so I wouldn't suffocate under the weight of it all.

When you left,

You took away,

The reason for my existence with you.

The time when I tried to survive by tracing lines on my wrist,

I found myself whispering.

"Life turns away from me,

And death denies me too,

Tell me, where am I to go?

These are nothing but traces of you..."

RESILIENCE OF HEART

You tell me, how do I turn around and let the memories leave
scars??

Even if time rewinds,

Even if I feel your blade whisper at my back,

I would never regret falling for you,

Though I know anything that falls, shatters...

DEATHBED..

It is said that when one lays upon their deathbed,

The mind replays the finest 7 minutes of their life.

My seven minutes??

He stole them.

When I'll lay on my deathbed, he might be the one whom I see,

I see nothing but a cascade of memories,

Fleeting glimpse of our shared moments,

Echoes of laughter and whispers of love...

8. ......

•47•

<u>SPECIAL THEME</u>

Counting years of memories,

I still wait for you.

Even if it means falling,

Into fate's relentless view...

BROKEN

STRINGS

BROKEN STRINGS

STOLEN TIME

Our separation is written by fate,

Yet I refused to accept this weight.

I steal you from time, to make you mine.

Our decorated dream, a radiant stream,

Escaping like a fleeting beam.

This is not the time, but still, I wait—

A night will come, and change our fate.

In another universe, hearts intertwined,

You and I together, a love redefined...

UNTAMED TOMORROW

Searching for solace in a new tomorrow,

Grant me a corner within your heart,

Let me become a small yet cherished part.

For you, I left the world behind,

Forsaking all, my ties unlined.

Oh babe, the depth of love I bear,

Is a devotion beyond of what you're aware.

I drink to drown the weight of sorrow,

And then, as if by fate, you appear before me.

I whisper softly,

"Let's drift away,

Where time itself begins to fade,

Where moments freeze, and hearts remain,

And tomorrow's dawn is but a dream, untamed..."

LINGERING REGRETS

I can't believe you're really gone,

I still see us walking that path,

Your hand in mine, your laughter echoing—

It feels so real, but it's just a memory now.

Those momentary sparks, once vibrant and bright,

Now lie in shadows, swallowed by night.

I want to forget the world in your embrace,

To find solace in the warmth of your grace.

I hate myself, the pain won't fade,

For failing you, for choices made.

That night still haunts my fragile mind,

Your absence cruel, the world unkind.

My shattered heart can't find the sun,

These broken shards now pierce my chest.

"My life is gone, swallowed by your dread,

Yet here I stand, though you're the one dead..."

TIMELESS GRACE OF LOVE..

If fate could grant me one more chance,

If time could turn its course,

I'd give my life to change your path,

And shield you from remorse.

You were the only light to my dim life and I'll do anything to change your fate,

Even if it means falling into the vortex of fate.

Don't ask how much I suffered, just smile,

Your smile just makes all the sufferings disappear.

When I am gone, roam freely, love,

Embrace life's vibrant grace;

Solve riddles by the lantern's glow,

And feel the ocean's trace.

Taste every sweet the world can give,

And I'll be there, close by—

"A Ruyi Flower at your side,

As years and dreams drift by,

I'll love you till the end of the moon,

Till the end of the universe, till the end of me..."

WHEN THE MOON FADE TO ASH

I held you, but it was too late,

Your last words, just my name.

Funny how I believed you would be fine, but the world, the very
one I saved time and time again, had to be cruel to us.

The heart that once echoed with the most malicious sound fell
silent,

How iconic, how tragic, that I begged you to stay, even though
Satan had already claimed you for a better place.

And I refused to accept that you were gone,

I saved the world, but couldn't save mine,

Now, I drink sorrow from my wine.

I lost you, I'm all alone now.

Without you, I've perished,

I've vanished, In your love, I've been diminished.

"This is the end of you and me,

A love that ended before it could breathe..."

......

Now I'm left alone,

Standing in a nice dress, staring at you leaving,

Leaving behind all the dreams we were weaving,

*While the shadow of death lingers, stealing
what's left of meaning...*

Maybe you left because I wasn't enough,

Loving me, for you, was just too tough...

WRITE WHAT YOU FEEL..

Journey

Journey of Writing This Masterpiece

As I reflect on the immense joy of publishing my debut poetry book, I feel compelled to share the process of its creation.

There were countless sleepless nights, far more than I can count on my fingers. During those moments, self-doubt crept in—would readers truly connect with my words? At times, the weight of it all felt too much, and I seriously considered backing out. Balancing my sports commitments with a heavy ankle injury, upcoming exams, schoolwork, and holiday homework made everything seem overwhelming.

But despite it all, I have my best friend to thank for being my constant pillar of support. My best friend listened, remained calm, and motivated me to keep going when I thought I couldn't continue.

There were moments when I cried after reading my own poems, moved by the raw emotion within them. To find inspiration, I often turned to Chinese dramas with heartbreaking endings and Marvel movies, marveling at the depth of their stories. In a way, these poems carry pieces of my own life—my struggles, my triumphs, and my emotional journey.

I started writing poems for this b

There will not be any sequels of this book. If you want to read more poems of mine please go to _wordsby_aditi in Instagram, further updates will be available there.

With Love,

Aditi

Upcomming Novel

BENEATH THE SKATES

Genres - Sports, Injuries, Depression, Betrayl, High School, Dystopian, Found Family

Selene Beth's life revolves around the ice until a tragic injury forces her to step away from her dreams. Struggling to find a new will to live, her world shifts in unexpected ways, meeting someone who turned her life 360. Selene learns that the path to healing is as unpredictable as the ice itself.

Stay Tunned in my Instagram for further updates.

_wordsby_aditi

Again with love,

Aditi

About The Author

Hey everyone, I am Aditi, the author of this book. I was born on August 22, 2008, in India. Writing has always been my passion, and through my stories, I explore themes of love, destiny, and heartbreak. I enjoy creating complex characters and weaving emotional, fantastical worlds that resonate with my readers. When I'm not writing, I find inspiration in music and the emotions it brings. I'm excited to share my journey with you through my stories and hope they touch your hearts as much as they've touched mine.